FROGS IN PRINCE CLOTHING

A Book of Poetry

Stella B James

Cover designed by Carrie Yarbrough

This book is a work of fiction. Names, characters, places, and incidents either are products of the author's imagination or are used fictitiously. Any resemblance to actual persons, living or dead, events, or locales is entirely coincidental.

Stella B James
Visit my Instagram @stellabjames

Printed in the United States of America

First Printing: April 2019

ISBN-9781095268551

To my amazing husband who turned out to be the Happily Ever After I had been searching for.

They say, "Beware of the wolf who lays hidden in sheep's clothing." I tell you, "Beware of the frog who lays hidden in the clothing of a prince."

—STELLA B JAMES

Stella B James

THE BEGINNING

It started with one
her first young love.
He charmed his way
into her heart
with his sweet words
and desperate declarations.
But when he sang
that very tune
to some other girl,
she realized she had
been played the fool.
How I wish I could have
warned her that he was
simply one of many.
There were much
more yet to come.

Would my young self
have heeded my warning?

Star Gazing

As I lay in the grass
behind the houses
full of life,
I look up into
the stars and galaxy mysteries
we often lost ourselves in.
I stretch out my hand
and feel the cold empty
spot beside me.
And I wish we had tried.

I wish we had never given in.

The Middle

"Meet me at our spot".

I tip toed through
my sleepy house.
Dodged the creaky
parts of my worn
porch steps.
Walked down
the darkened street
highlighted by the
flickering street lamps.
And I met you
at the middle,
halfway between our homes,
our unspoken desires,
our desperate hearts,
silently beating out
each other's name.

That Last Summer

I can still smell
the humid summer air
that wafted through the
open windows of your
beat up truck.

I can still hear
the carefree laugh
that bubbled up from
your happy soul
as the bumps jostled us closer.

I can still feel
the callouses of your
hard worked fingers
as they slid across the seat
and latched onto mine.

I could never forget our last summer.

I Wonder...

what if I hadn't left
if I hadn't answered the phone
hadn't cried until I was hoarse
hadn't let you find me
hadn't climbed into your lap
hadn't believed she meant nothing
that she was just a friend
hadn't let you kiss me goodbye
hadn't waited for you to call

If I hadn't done all these things,
would my feelings have been spared
seeing you now, with her?

Yours

How that one
simple pronoun
can make all
the difference
in my world.

There

She is always there.
When you need her,
and when you don't.
When you're busy,
or all alone.
When you hate her,
or love her too much.
When you wish she
would just forget you,
but you're glad that she won't.
When you're lost,
and full of self-hate.
When she tries to save you,
but you push her away.
When she breaks down,
and begs for you to try.
When you wish you could
make her smile instead of cry.
When she says she's done,
but she still comes back.
When she promises she's okay,
but her voice starts to crack.
She is always there.

Smiles

She lived a life
of fakes smiles
until she met you
and survived
the real thing.

Now she can
hardly contain herself.

First Love Magic

He didn't wake her
from eternal slumber,
or save her from
an evil queen.
He didn't find her
in a lonely tower,
or as a being
of the sea.
She had no spells,
no fairies or elves,
and she couldn't
dance or sing.
But she was his princess,
and he, her prince.
And though theirs
wasn't a happily ever after
fairy tale ending,
they still shared
the magic of first love.

Spinning

You turn me
inside out
and outside in,
upside down,
this way and that,
round and round.

You leave me breathless,
mindless, and confused.
I never knew it'd feel
this way by simply
falling head over heels for you.

Have. Are. Will.

I wound my fingers
through your curls
and gripped them tight,
if only for you to feel
a fraction of the pain
you have caused me,
are causing me,
will cause me.

Breathless

"Save your breath," he said.
"I plan on stealing it later."

Little did he know that
she had remained breathless
from the moment they met.

Same Old Excuse

"Because I love him"
seemed to excuse
his every bad deed.

"Because I love him"
kept her forever
in great need.

"Because I love him"
never meant to him
a damned thing.

"Because I love him"
held her heart afloat
while her soul left drowning.

Can We

Can we live in the moment
we fell in love
and saw no other possibilities
without one another?

Can we pretend that tomorrow
will never come to pass,
that this fragile love
might have a chance to last?

Can we just be?

Truly. Madly. Deeply.

She believed in fairy tale love
the truly, madly, deeply kind.
And she found a boy
who promised his heart.
He *truly* wanted her
for the rest of his days.
He *madly* oppressed her,
locking her in a cage.
He *deeply* hurt her,
refusing to set her free.

He was never prepared
to fall in love
with a wild thing.

Tell Me

Tell me again.
About how we
fell in love.

Tell me what
we said and
how we felt.

Tell me how
we were forever,
and then explain
why we're not.

Floating Scraps

And with shaky hands
I tore every letter.
I burned the pile
of shredded scraps
and watched your
broken promises
float away with the wind.

Love Never Stops

For what it's worth
she loved you until the end,
even when she said she didn't.
Even when she swore
she never wanted to see you again,
she loved you.
When she refused to never
speak to you,
she loved you.
Even months after,
she loved you.

Even now,
she still loves you.

Before

Love was
so simple
before the
pain of
heartbreak.

Metamorphosis

Somewhere in between
Barbies and braces,
Saturday morning cartoons
and movie dates,
grass stained jeans
and little black dresses,
comics and angsty novels,
Chapstick and mascara,
cooties and make out sessions,
she had developed into
what little boys respected
and what grown men longed for.

She became Woman.

The Heart Learns

Heartache is a pain
in which the broken
pieces shift back
into place,
little by little,
sealing the fissures
with discovered lessons
and learning to beat
again on its own.

Irresistible You

He had a Lennon nose,
with Jagger lips
and Leto smoulder.
Springsteen curls,
with a Bruno smile
and a James Dean aura.
An Elvis sway,
with a Dylan attitude,
and a Sinatra croon.

I never stood a chance.

Date Night In

Cigarette smoke
and cheap red wine
Melty wax stubs
and record player scratches
Muted television
and a shared fuzzy blanket.

A typical night
in my apartment
alone with him.

Unrequited Love at the Jukebox

A5 I'm Yours
B1 Free Bird
D6 You're the One that I Want
C4 The Wanderer
A7 All You Need is Love
D2 In My Own Time
E3 One Way or Another
D9 You Can't Always Get What You Want
A2 Surrender
B6 You Can't Hurry Love
E1 Take My Breath Away
C3 Under Pressure
B8 Don't Worry Baby
E10 Born to be Wild
C5 I Will Survive

Falling Again

Whatever she used to believe,
she doesn't anymore.
She can't afford
the false sense of hope.

She fell in love once,
and it smashed her to bits.
She swore to never
fall in or out of love again.

No, she refuses to fall,
so she scales the rocky
edges of love instead,
tethered by logic and reason.

But with one look
and many promises kept,
she cut her cord and happily
plummeted into love's abyss.

I Get It– You Aren't Him

Stop telling me
that you are not him.
He said the very same.
Stop telling me
with you will be different.
Stop giving it another name.
Show me your truth,
your worthiness,
your so called loyalty.
Let your gestures speak
the things I refuse to hear,
but please stop telling me.

Walking After Crutches

He saw a side of her
created out of bitter heartbreak.
In her weaker moments,
she would pledge her love.
He saw through her declarations,
saw her already crushed spirit.
Maybe she used him,
but he allowed it.
Loving her was his weakness,
one he soon came to despise.
He claimed to be her crutch,
yet she was his sling.
Two beings unable to tear away
from mending the broken things.
Yes, he was her crutch,
yet she gladly hobbled away.

Body Language

It never mattered,
that our tongues
spoke a different language.
Not when we had our eyes
that read between the lines.
Or our fingers
that would intertwine.
Or our mouths,
that savoured the
taste of our skin.
Or our limbs,
that we found
ourselves wrapped within.
Our tongues never needed the words
our bodies were already able to speak.

Eurotrash

It was his charm
in the beginning.
Those big, brown eyes
with their hint of mischief.
Or maybe, it was how
easily he towered over her.
How he cupped her
face for each kiss,
or how he danced with her
on darkened streets.
It was the way he would
laugh off the little things,
and ignore the bigger ones.
Or the way he would forget
to call her back when he got home,
if he ever did get home.
It was the way her heart
clenched when she saw him
sitting with someone new.
The desperate sound of her name.
She swore never again,
but here she is,
pouring his morning coffee.

Hurt So Good

Everything about him
was exquisitely painful.
The way his fingers
would tangle in her hair.
Or how he would
squeeze her to him
until she was smothered
up against him,
lungs begging to be refilled.
His bruising kisses
would leave her raw,
desperate for more.
And the way he let
her slip from his heart
was by far the most
exquisite pain of all.

Stained

She wore red lipstick,
and black mascara every day.

She liked the way they left their own stains;
one of lust, the other of ache.

Both for the man she would never have.

Lost Sensibilities

Why do we lie to ourselves
for a love that is just as untrue?

Despite Everything

I have
fallen for you,
loved you,
cried over you,
hated you,
lost you,
missed you,
forgiven you.

All these things,
but I can't forget you.

To Be the One

He watched her.
Watched how her
hair flowed around her
as she swayed and twirled.
Watched how her eyes closed
and her lips spread into a smile.
Watched as she leaned into
the unknown boy behind her.
And he felt his heart twist,
and wished he was that boy.
Wished he would get
the courage to sway with her.
To be the one her eyes settled on
when she opened them back up.
To be the one who could
make her smile like a Rolling Stones song.

To simply be the one.

I See You

"What happened to you?"

He looked over himself,
at his crisp button down shirt,
his large, calloused hands.
He looked fine,
seemed fine,
and he looked up
at her in confusion.
She shook her head,
and stepped closer to him.

"That's not what I meant."
She opened his shirt
and placed her hand
over his heart.

"Here. What happened to
you in here?"

Blue

Your eyes were
the deepest shade of blue,
so much so, that I
wished to grow a
mermaid's tail
and dive into the
deepest depths,
right down to
your volcanic soul.

Hardened Heart

I knew this boy,
not quite a man,
who loved with his heart
sewn to his sleeve.
Those girls, they ripped at it,
its edges they frayed,
until he could take no more
and sought out a reprieve.

I met this boy
years later to the day,
and he bragged to be a man
who no longer fell as quick.
He forgot how love could feel
and that heart he used to display
now remains patchworked
under skin made thick.

His

She could be sweet,
demure, and innocent.
She could be cynical,
intelligent, and sarcastic.
She could be wicked,
tempting, and sensual.
She could be rowdy,
silly, and spontaneous.
She could be crazed,
erratic, and depressed.
She could be furious,
vindictive, and unforgiving.
She could be humble,
sincere, and trusting.

But above all else–
despite the things
she could be–
she *was* his.

Red and Black

Red and Black
hers and his
silken strands intermingled
on a stark white pillow.

Red and Black
passion filled eyes
of blind adoration
and unbridled lust.

Red and Black
opposing hearts;
One bleeding love,
the other already dead.

If

If...
what a promising little word.
But if what?
What a deceiving little beast.

Salt and Merlot

And this wine does
nothing for me,
but coat my tongue
in all the truths
I'd never admit
to you otherwise.
They spill from
my traitorous lips
and mix in with
the salt of my tears.

Salt and Merlot.

Was the combination
something you enjoyed?

Fallen

If I was your angel,
then you alone
dragged me down
from paradise to hell
where I now remain fallen,
hoping my frayed wings
will one day fly again.

The Beast

And maybe I'm the one
who broke my heart in the end.
I saw too much good in you
that was never really there.
I put the words in your mouth
that I wanted to hear.
I made excuses for your cruelty,
tried to believe you a tragic soul.
You warned me in the beginning,
but I just had to believe.
Afterall, doesn't the Beauty
usually break the Beast?

We Keep On

Everything keeps on.

Whatever the obstacles,
whether held back
or knocked down,
we keep on.

Despite the loss,
the regret
or the pain,
we keep on.

No matter the
broken promises,
or deep heartache,
we keep on.

Even though I
caught you watching me,
you turned and continued
on your way.

Everything keeps on.

Your Everything

You–
your laugh,
your touch,
your smile,
your voice,
your taste,
your smell–
everything that is you,
she has forgotten.
But not the pain.
The pain you caused her
is a constant dull ache
in the deepest recesses
of her fractured heart.

Monsters

She believed in
shooting stars
and majestic castles
in the sky.
Of love at first sight
and happily ever after's.
Of second chances,
and hard fought redemption.

But he showed her
the beauty in the
fearsome things.
That not all monsters
hide in closets or under beds.
That, more often than not,
they are created.
And sometimes,
most times,
only a love like hers can save them.

My Constant

You loved me
when I was a
simple sweet girl
living out fairy tale wishes.

And again,
when I was lonely
and desperately clinging
to something true.

And again,
when I was left
bitter and scorned,
unable to believe anymore.

You loved me
as I drifted further
from your promising
outstretched hand.

And through it all,
you never changed
from the boy I met
to the man I left.

You always stayed the same.

Heat

All she felt
when he came near
was indescribable heat.
His stare melted her,
his touch scorched her,
his words singed her,
his kiss set fire to her veins.
She would gladly
be reduced to ashes
as long as it was him
she burned for.

Daytime Strangers

They lived for the night.
For the breaths they shared,
the synchronized beating
of their frantic hearts.
The moonlight crazed them,
allowing them a moment
to forget that they had
nothing in common.
That they lived in two very
different realities.
That in the light of the sun,
they were practically strangers.
But in his darkened room,
he knew her best.

Follow Your Heart

If you find your heart wandering,
don't leash it or fence it in.
These unpredictable things
are meant to explore and discover.
If your heart is on an exploration,
one that you'd least expect,
it may be leading you out
of the undesirable towards
a place you'd never considered before.

And it could make all the difference.
So in short, follow your heart.

Shared Quiet

In the quiet moments,
where you can feel
a heart beating
and hear steady breathing–
those are the moments
you are truly sharing
with someone.

Question

If we only want
what we can't have,
then how is it
that I still want you
after all this time?

Drowning

I once believed him
to be my anchor.
But he kept pulling me under.

Obedience School

His tongue knew tricks
unlike any other–
the greatest convincing me
our love was something eternal.

Sit. Stay. Play dead.
Good heart.

Blindfolded

I was so blind,
but how could I help myself?
Your promises, your declarations
your secrets, your lies
your double worded snares–
all woven together
in and out, over and under
into one intricate blindfold
thickened by all your words
I so desperately clung to.

A blindfold I wore like a second skin
and you tightened the knot
a little more each day.

Just Me

Call me every name
you wish me to be.
I can't be her,
or them,
of long loves past
but I will always
love you as
plain old me.

Will that ever be enough?

What We Had

Love can be
a beautifully painful thing.
But this destruction
you have bestowed upon me--
Darling, that is not love.

I'll never know what it was.

Battle Cry

My mind says, *no*,
but my heart begs, *please.*

My mind demands,
Never forget
while my heart soothes,
But always forgive.

My mind fears the worst,
my heart hopes for the best.

My mind aches,
my heart does too.
Each constantly at war
when it comes to you.

Singed

She couldn't explain
why she always returned to him.
She knew it made her
look silly, or weak,
or whatever else they
called her behind her back.
But what they could never
understand was that she
had no control over it.
She was drawn to him
in a way that was beyond her,
much like the moth
is drawn to the flame.

And her precious wings
singe a little more each time.

Calling the Devil

How many times
have I called
out your name
in the most
desolate moments
of my life
only to remind
myself that you
are the cause
of this acute hopelessness.

Puppet Master

I served as the marionette
of your master puppet show.
Every word I spoke,
every move I made,
all for your approval.

I do hope your
fingers are sore
after playing my
strings for so long.

Balloons

We're as committed
as balloons held
captive by tight fists.

Pieces

She wanted to break.
She longed for the pain.
She wanted the pieces
to belong to him.
If only to feel
that some part of it
was indeed true,
even if only to her.

Midnight Calls

The shadows on my wall,
they resembled you
in such a way
that I had to
reach for my phone
and call you up
to make sure
you were really gone.

Sorry for waking you.

Healing

The mind tells the heart
what it refuses to believe.
It isn't the mind that breaks,
and maybe the heart knows
a little more about resiliency.
The mind tries to protect,
the heart refuses to accept.
Not unlike the parent
shielding their child
who seeks to rebel and run wild.
But the mind forgives,
welcomes the heart back in.
"It will be okay in the end,"
it whispers, hoping the heart
believes in the things
the mind cannot accept.

Vultures

My heart prefers to play
blind, deaf, and dumb
if it means keeping
you for just a bit longer.

Feed it more lies.
Come on, fatten it up.
Don't vultures prefer
a little meat on their prey?

Run

They say she
left him.

She says
it was more
like an escape.

Happy

And I am happy for her.

They complement each other well.
They will build each other up.
They will never go to bed mad.
They will love each other through it all.

She won't drive him crazy
with her insecurities.
She won't smother him
with her affection.
She won't frustrate him
with her forgetfulness.
She won't lessen herself
to feel worthy of him.

I tell myself this.
I make myself see.
She will never be the me
I was with you.

And I am happy for her.

The Kind of Love that Lasts

It's heartbreak that can shut us down,
that can harden us up,
and make it so that no one else
will get close enough to hurt us.
But in that self-protection,
we end up hurting ourselves more.
It's a lonely existence,
shutting ourselves away
and keeping everyone else at bay.
Trust is hard, but necessary
for things like love and companionship.
Honesty can seem even harder,
until you meet that someone
that just naturally pulls it out of you.
And stays for the ugly bits
that no one else has ever seen.
You save all that for true love,
for that kind of love is the only kind
that sustains and thrives.

Scars

Scars are forever, my dear,
and you are the deepest one.

A long, jagged, hideous thing,
that runs from the memories
in the back of my mind,
to the lips you kissed goodnight,
to the hands you clasped tight,
to the heart you deceived,
to the very soul you denied its mate.
And though you disappeared,
it will never go away.

Scars are forever, my dear,
and I hope to be your deepest one.

Pawns

I know you are with her,
just as you know I am with him.
And we are happy.

Yes, we are happy.
They are safe.
They aren't toxic.

Toxic–
like the way you consume me.
Toxic–
like the way I won't allow you to forget.
Toxic–
like the never ending games we play.

I know you are with her,
just as you know I am with him.
Our pathetic little pawns.

And we are happy.

I Never Loved You.

Maybe if I say it enough,
I'll come to believe it.

I never loved you.
I never loved you.
I never loved you.
I never loved you.
I never loved you.
I never loved you.
I never loved you.

A mantra for each day.
I inhale every word,
exhale each syllable,
and pray it will take root
in the universe somewhere.

I never loved you.
I never loved you.
I never loved you.

Sometimes lying to ourselves
is the only way we can overcome.

I never loved you.

For a Reason

Sometimes,
you aren't meant to be.

Sometimes,
they teach you things–
some lessons good,
others bad.

And sometimes,
after you have fallen
in love and settled down,
you will look back
and see that those
people who weren't meant
to belong to you
still played an integral role
in helping you
prepare your heart
for the one who
would ultimately
capture it and
cherish it for all time.

The Storm Within

She's more destructive
than you know.
A tsunami of emotions,
A tornado of passion,
A flood of sorrow,
An earthquake of fury.
But when she smiles,
it is brighter than the
sun on a cloudless day.
And just to glimpse her
rainbow makes all
her torrential mood swings
a little less terrifying.

Ghost Trail

Walk a little further
into my memories past.
Can you withstand the haunted trail
of the ones who couldn't last?
Will you learn from their mistakes,
make a few of your own?
Will you be the one I keep forever,
the one I can finally call my home?

On and On

And he said,
"I'm not looking for
a relationship right now."
"Good," I replied,
"neither am I."

And that should have
been the end of what
was supposed to be us.

But we just kept on happening.

Winking

I know that I am supposed
to hate when a guy
winks my way.
And I'm supposed to scoff
aloud and call him a pig.
He does it again,
in this house
full of people.
We are out back,
and he is on the phone.
His eyes meet mine,
a small smile comes
to his lips before he does it.
I should hate it,
but then, why does
my heart flutter
and my cheeks stain red?
Only for him,
for eyeing the one
thing in this crowded place
that longs to be
the centre of his universe.
And is.

Bound Hearts

Her heart never belonged to her.
It had always been his.
From the moment
it took its first beat,
it pumped for him.
It soared with his successes
and broke with his pain.
It longed for his touch,
and knew every letter to his name.
It belonged to him
without his knowledge,
and when finally found,
he took that heart
and worshipped it fully
for to her heart
his own beating heart
was eternally bound.

Splatters

His words splattered over me,
the meaning sinking into my skin.
And I am left stained
by those cruel synonyms.
I can't bear to let you see me,
for what he says that I am,
and will never be.
But you kissed me deep,
and wiped me clean
with your belief that
I am something
too extraordinary for
a mere mortal's tongue.

The Me Without You

I can't say
I regret it all,
but I'll never
find myself missing it.
Maybe you were
an integral part
to helping me reach
where I am now
but you'll never get the credit
for who I am now.
I came to this point
despite your harsh words,
and despite what you said
I'd never be without you.
I find myself here,
in a better life,
with a better man,
because you never believed that I could.

I do revel in how you loathe being proven wrong.

Character You Play

You aren't merely
a chapter in her book,
a quick insignificant appearance.
You are the climatic part,
and it is up to you
whether you will turn out to be
the hero or the villain.

U-G-L-Y

I'll take on your ugly,
just as you've taken on mine.
And I will make you just as beautiful
as you have made me - inside and out.

Heroes

I have slayed my own dragons
more times than I can count.
But you banished the evil queen
setting those things to destroy me.

My hero.

Untamed

Do not seek to tame her,
to domesticate her.
Do not cut her down
to fit her like a potted plant.
Let her run free.
Let her roots grow.
Become the moon she chases,
the soil that strengthens her.

Become the thing she seeks
and could never live without.

Simple Man

You think yourself
a simple man.
My love,
there is no such thing.
To love a girl,
and turn her into
the woman I am,
takes more than
the heart of a
mere simple man.

Shape Me

You took my glob of clay
and formed me into a vase
so that I may hold all the love
you pour into me each day.

Thick and Thin

Thick and thin.
He has stood by me
through it all.

Thick and thin.
He has caught me
for every stumble and fall.

Thick and thin.
He has celebrated my good,
and forgiven my bad.

Thick and thin.
He too isn't perfect,
but he's the best I've ever had.

To Be Loyal

Loyalty.
It's the thing
I loved about him,
but he hated in me.
I loved how
he stood by those
that he admired most.
And he hated how
I stood by those
that hurt me most.

What did that say about us then?

Read Between the Eyes

Her eyes held all the secrets
her lips would never spill.
Her words were nothing
but a naughty little thrill.

She led them on
with little remorse.
Broken promises
to keep them on course.

One day a boy will see
through all the tales and lies.
He'll take the time to read
the passage of her eyes.

And only then will her heart be known.

Soulmates

He wants us to love like them,
to live as they did.
They had a true love,
the truest he'd ever seen.
I think they call that
soulmates, my darling.

We have nothing to worry about.

Rise and Fall

Love keeps me here.
My sanity keeps me away.
The heart often convinces
the mind that our madness
is what keeps us alive.
Alive and thriving,
and driving us to bitter depths
and soaring heights.

I'll shoot up to the stars
as fast as I will
plummet to the ground.
All for you.

Forever for you.

Evergreen

Long ago are the days
I was a mere wilted flower.
You have made me evergreen.

Wild

I've never liked the idea
that we belong to someone.
I don't want to belong,
to be collared and noosed.
I want to run rampant,
to explore and to dream.
I'd rather a pack,
a mate of my own.
And together we'll run
and howl our freedom,
our victory song.

Backspace

Imissyousomuch
thatIcan'tevenafford
thespacesinbetweenthesewords
asitcreatestoomuchvoidbetweenus.

Broke

If I had a dollar
for every time that
you let me down,
I would be a peasant
among the others
collecting their debts
from lesser men.

Keys

You were locked up tight,
and I had no key.
Did someone steal it away?
Had you hidden it,
buried it deep
where no one had hope
of finding it?

I have never been
celebrated for my patience.
I didn't need a key.
I had a crowbar,
and little by little,
inch by inch,
I pried you open.

Out tumbled that
fabled key and
we both took one look at it
before kicking it aside.
What need have we
for locks and keys
with nothing left to hide?

Our Seasons

You were Spring
in my dead
of Winter.
You breathed life
into my frozen being,
my heart thawing,
my reservations melting.
I basked in your
Summer touches,
your refreshing showers,
your sweet redemption.
And I changed with your Autumn,
let those unwanted parts of me
brown and crumble.
I don't fear Winter
this time around.
Not when you are
the chill that nips
my frosted lips
and sweeps across
my bare limbs.
Not when knowing
that our seasons
mark us as something
eternal and everchanging.

Of My Dreams

I dreamt that we had never met,
that I was free to be with whoever I chose.
But in that dream,
I sought you out.
You see, now that I have found you,
I can't see myself with anyone else.
You are quite literally
the man of my dreams.

Two

My heart beats
in two syllables.

Prince Charming

Something.
He has something
I can't quite explain.
Something that drew me in,
and it keeps me here still.
Something that I must
have seen from the moment
I laid my eyes on him.
He's just got that something,
and he himself is quite something.
Something was all I needed
in the end.

To my family, friends, and
Instagram Followers,
I thank you for encouraging
me to write this.

ABOUT THE AUTHOR

Stella B. James is a Southern girl who enjoys strong coffee, dry martinis, and sharing her poetry on Instagram, mostly about love and the angst that follows falling out of love. In *Frogs in Prince Clothing*, she shares those past experiences with you.

Made in the USA
Middletown, DE
06 November 2019

78062967R00066